W9-AXV-732

JOHN DONOVAN LIBRARY
MADISON CENTRAL SCHOOL
Madison, New York 1 42

tECHiES

Steve Jobs

Steve Jobs

{ Thinks Different }

ANN BRASHARES

TWENTY-FIRST CENTURY BOOKS

BROOKFIELD, CONNECTICUT

For Sam, proud owner of a birthday-blue iMac.

Thanks to Jean Reynolds, Jason Altman, Rebecca Archibald, Russell Gordon, Lauren Monchik, Chris Grassi, Nicole Greenblatt, and Lynne Amft

Special thanks to Bradley Wellington for contributing "Tech Talk"

Design by Lynne Amft

Produced by 17th Street Productions,
an Alloy Online, Inc. company
33 West 17th Street, New York, NY 10011

© 2001 by Twenty-First Century Books. All rights reserved. Published by Twenty-First Century Books, a Division of The Millbrook Press, Inc. Printed in Hong Kong.

17th Street Productions and the 17th Street Productions logo are trademarks and/or registered trademarks of Alloy Online, Inc. Twenty-First Century Books and the Twenty-First Century logo are trademarks of The Millbrook Press, Inc.

Library of Congress Cataloging-in-Publication Data
Brashares, Ann.
Steve Jobs: thinks different / by Ann Brashares.
p. cm.
Includes index.
ISBN 0-7613-1959-X (lib. bdg.)
1. Jobs, Steven, 1955- —Juvenile literature. 2. Businesspeople—Biography—Juvenile literature. 3. Computer industry—United States—Juvenile literature. 4. Apple Computer, Inc.—Juvenile literature. [1. Jobs, Steven, 1955- 2. Businesspeople. 3. Computer industry. 4. Apple Computer, Inc.] I. Title.

HD9696.2.U62 J633   2001
338.7'6100416'092—dc21   00-057706
                              [B]

lib: 10 9 8 7 6 5 4 3 2 1

contents

{ CHAPTER ONE }

Growing Up in the Valley

Sand and Fruit

IN 1955 THE SILICON OF SILICON VALLEY WAS STILL JUST SAND, AND THE SUN-BAKED VALLEY FLOOR WAS COVERED WITH APRICOT ORCHARDS AND CHERRY GROVES. THE PRETTY, QUIET LOWLAND BETWEEN THE BIG CALIFORNIA CITIES OF SAN FRANCISCO AND SAN JOSE WASN'T YET THE WORLD'S CAPITAL OF HIGH TECHNOLOGY. IT WAS A SLEEPY, RURAL PLACE, EDEN BEFORE THE APPLE—AN IDYLLIC SPOT TO GROW UP. ESPECIALLY IF YOU LOVE EATING FRUIT.

STEVEN PAUL JOBS WAS BORN IN THE HEART OF THAT

valley in 1955, and he adores fruit—cherries, plums . . . apples. Turns out he has a pretty healthy appetite for sand, too. Not for eating, but for making silicon, the stuff that paved the trail for the speed-racing digital revolution. His revolution.

And like any revolution, there are things you gain and things you lose. The Santa Clara Valley gained a catchy new name, miles of industrial parks, office complexes and asphalt, loads of money, and worldwide fame. It gained Apple Computer, fruit of one sort, you could say. But it lost most of its orchards, fruit of another.

Adopted as a small baby by Paul and Clara Jobs of Mountain View, California, Jobs grew up in a ranch-style house with his parents and his younger sister, Patricia. His father worked as a machinist for a company that made lasers, and his mother worked as a school secretary. His parents were hardworking, but the Jobs family never had much extra money.

Jobs said his father was a "genius with his hands." Paul Jobs bought used cars from a junkyard, fixed them, and sold them at a profit. "That was my college fund," Jobs explained to a *New York Times* writer. Jobs spent many childhood hours with his father, scouring junkyards for old car parts and cast-off treasures.

It was a growing tradition in the valley, even in the mid-1960s, for electronics hobbyists to make workshops in their garages and spend weekends fooling with oscillators and other relics. Jobs had the privilege of peeking in on his neighbors' work. Though he's been described as a withdrawn kid, he was never afraid to ask questions. He took from these suburban garages a lifelong fascination with electronics.

Jobs was a smart kid, capable of intense focus when he was interested in something, but he wasn't always a good student. He was actually kicked out of his fourth-grade class for acting up with the teacher. But this turned out to be a lucky break. Jobs landed in a new class with a teacher who understood how to motivate him: bribery. She literally promised him money if he did his work. And did he ever do his work. He did so much work that he skipped fifth grade completely.

Junior high wasn't so easy. Crittenden Junior High was a chaotic, even dangerous school, and Jobs hated it so much that he actually convinced his parents to move. The family moved to Sunnyvale, with its safer, better junior high school.

At thirteen, Jobs's interest in electronics was blossoming. One day he was building an electronic counting machine, and he needed some parts. He knew he could get them from Hewlett-Packard, a giant electronics company not far from his house. Jobs looked up the phone number of Bill Hewlett, the cofounder of Hewlett-Packard. Some kids would have been afraid to dial up one the richest and most important men in California. Not Steve Jobs.

He boldly chatted with Bill Hewlett for twenty minutes, and Hewlett was so impressed and surprised by the young man that he not only gave him the parts he needed but offered him a summer job, too. That phone call taught an early lesson: If you ask for what you want, you often get it.

Two Steves

There was another boy, a few years older, who lived in Sunnyvale. He was also interested in electronics and was also named Steve—Steve Wozniak, known to his friends as "Woz." Steve Wozniak and Steve Jobs became friends. "Woz was the first person I met who knew more about electronics than I did," Jobs later said.

While Woz went to college at Berkeley and Jobs attended Homestead High School, they worked on a prank project. Together they made and sold "blue boxes," special homemade devices that allowed users to make free long-distance telephone calls anywhere in the world. Legend has it that Woz once pretended to be Secretary of State Henry Kissinger and called the pope at the Vatican—toll-free, of course. This was a mischievous (okay, illegal) little business, but it showed the two Steves that they made an excellent team—Woz as the engineer and Jobs as the motivator and salesman.

This wasn't their only weird moneymaking scheme. For a short time the two of them dressed up as characters from *Alice in Wonderland* to entertain children outside a shopping mall. They traded off playing the White Rabbit and the Mad Hatter. Jobs hated it. At least it was legal.

In 1972, Jobs graduated from high school. He thought about going to Stanford University in nearby Palo Alto but said of the place, "Everyone there knew what they wanted to do with their lives. And I didn't know what I wanted to do with my life at all." Instead he enrolled at Reed College in Portland, Oregon. But he wasn't happy there. He dropped out of his classes after less than a year, though he continued to float around campus, picking apples and soaking up the raging youth culture of the early 1970s.

The late 1960s and early 1970s were a famous time of change and rebellion in America. Millions of teenage baby boomers like Jobs wanted to reinvent the world in their image. They wore jeans instead of coats and ties; they listened to rock music, the louder the better. They grew their hair long and mounted serious protests against the government—most urgently against the war in Vietnam. They demanded peace, freedom, and the pursuit of mind-bending experiences, and Steve Jobs was smack in the middle of it.

Jobs had more on his mind than just hanging around. He wanted to expand his horizons and direction. He traveled to India, seeking a guru. He lived in an ashram and learned about the Hindu religion. He became a vegetarian, an environmentalist, and a hippie—he grew a beard and let his hair get long and traveled barefoot wherever possible. According to legend, he ate only fruit and stopped taking showers.

His travels in India broadened his mind, but not in the way he had expected. Seeing the poverty, the sickness, and the primitive living conditions, Jobs later said that Thomas Edison had done more for the human condition than any guru.

It was time to get home, back to his former muse, electricity.

Returning to his hometown, Jobs got a job at Atari, the company that made the first-ever video game, called Pong, an electronic version of Ping-Pong that players at home could plug into their TV sets.

Jobs's old friend Woz was working as a junior engineer at Hewlett-Packard at the time, but Woz loved to visit Jobs at Atari in the evenings. They would spend all night playing arcade games for free. One time the founder of Atari, Nolan Bushnell, told the young friends he wanted a version of Pong that could be played by one user. Jobs said they could do it, and the two of them stayed up all night for four nights in a row. They worked so hard that they both got sick, but they succeeded. They created a game called Breakout, and thanks to the incredible skill of Woz, they did it with fewer parts than anyone at Atari imagined possible.

MITS Altair, the first personal computer

Homebrew

Jobs and Woz also spent time going to meetings of the Homebrew Computer Club, a group of gadget lovers who met every other Wednesday night to talk about the computers and electronic devices they built in their spare time.

In January 1975 the magazine *Popular Electronics* had announced the arrival of the first personal computer, called the Altair 8800. The Altair was a mail-order kit you assembled yourself. MITS, a company in Albuquerque, New Mexico, manufactured it. It had no keyboard, no monitor, and only 250 bytes of memory (compared to the more than 250 million bytes even the simplest computers have today). In fact, the Altair couldn't do much of anything until a couple of teenage hackers named Bill Gates (yes, that Bill Gates) and Paul Allen adapted a programming language for it, but the members of the Homebrew Computer Club were thrilled, anyway. The Altair was the first computer that a regular guy could buy and own.

Before 1975 computers were gigantic mainframes taking up entire rooms of the enormous companies and universities that owned them. Most of them were manufactured by the company IBM. These machines often cost as much as a million dollars and were used only by scientists and engineers. There was no such thing as a computer you could have on your desk at home or at an office.

For most members of Homebrew, the "microcomputer," as it was called then, was a fascinating hobby, but Steve Jobs saw it as something more. He wanted Woz to help him build a computer that was small and useful and simple enough that everybody in the world would want to have one. He imagined that even people who knew nothing about electronics could use it to write papers and figure out math problems and conduct experiments and play games. He believed that if he and Woz could build a computer like that it would change people's lives.

So that's exactly what they did.

JOHN DONOVAN LIBRARY
MADISON CENTRAL SCHOOL
Madison, New York 1 :402

CHAPTER TWO

Starting a Revolution

Are You Kidding?

In 1976, Steve Jobs and Steve Wozniak set up shop in the garage of the Jobses' family house in Los Altos, California. With a lot of excitement and a little money, the two friends began to build a computer. They named their tiny company Apple Computer and their first machine the Apple I.

Of the two Steves, Woz was the engineer. His friends in the Homebrew Club considered him a technical genius. The Apple I was based on a design that Woz had come up with to impress the gang at the Homebrew, using a microprocessor he had bought for twenty dollars at a computer show. A microprocessor is a chip of silicon (a substance known as a semiconductor because it conducts electricity and insulates it at the same time) inscribed with thousands or even millions of transistors (electronic devices used to control the flow of electricity in electronic equipment). The microchip serves as the brain of the computer. Like the Altair, you had to hook up the Apple I to your own monitor and keyboard, but it was simpler and more efficient than the Altair.

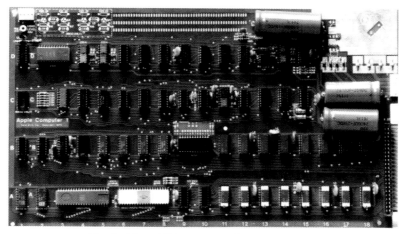

The insides of Woz's masterpiece, the Apple I

Woz's greatest talent was his ability to design electronic devices with fewer components—integrated circuits—than anyone else. He was practically a celebrity at Homebrew. For Woz it was like a puzzle. He took pride not only in solving it, but also in solving it in the simplest, shortest way possible.

While Woz was fascinated by the pure design of a computer, Jobs was more interested in finding a way to sell a lot of them.

There are different stories about how they came up with the name Apple. One story is that Steve Jobs loved the Beatles and named his company after the Beatles' Apple Records label. Another is that Jobs spent so much time picking apples when he lived in Oregon that he wanted to honor his favorite fruit. Most important, Jobs wanted a name for the company that would sound friendly and uncomplicated. He didn't want to scare regular people with the new technology. Apple did sound a lot friendlier than the names of the other computer companies at the time, like International Business Machines (IBM) or Microinstrumentation and Telemetry Systems (MITS). The story goes that the now-famous logo of the apple has a bite taken out of it so it wouldn't look like a cherry.

A lot of people, especially techies, thought the name Apple sounded silly for an electronics company. Others thought it seemed too cute. But, as usual, Steve Jobs's instincts were right on the money. That winning little apple became one of the best-known logos in the world.

Woz was still working at Hewlett-Packard at the time, so he needed to give his bosses the chance to develop the computer as an HP product. His bosses said no thanks. They didn't think these new "microcomputers" would ever be much of a success.

Steve Jobs breathed a huge sigh of relief when HP turned it down. But now they really were on their own. Woz sold his Hewlett-Packard programmable calculator, and Jobs sold his Volkswagen microbus, and they shelled out every bit of the resulting cash to pay for the parts to build their first computers.

Steve Jobs invited another engineer along for the ride, a man he and Woz knew from Atari named Ron Wayne. They didn't have any cash to pay him a salary, so they offered him 10 percent of the company instead. Soon after, Wayne became impatient about money and sold his 10 percent back to them for $300. If he had held on to his 10 percent stock in Apple, he would have had more than $65 million just four years later.

In 1976, Jobs and Wozniak sold 50 computers to an area store called the Byte Shop for $500 apiece, and their business was off and running.

In order to make Apple a big business, Jobs needed to raise more money to buy parts and equipment to build computers. Jobs made his pitch to banks and investors, but most businesspeople gaped in disbelief at the two hippies, Jobs hardly more than a teenager. Answers ranged from "no way" to "are you kidding?"

Finally, miraculously, Jobs met Mike Markkula. Markkula had worked for Intel, the largest chip-manufacturing company in the world, and made millions of dollars as Intel grew. Though he was only in his thirties, he had retired from Intel. When he met Jobs and Woz and saw the Apple II, he knew they were on the verge of something big. He gave them $91,000 of his own money and became the third partner in Apple Computer.

Another Technical Feat, Woz Style

Woz and Jobs were already at work on a better computer, the Apple II. Rather than being sold as a kit like other personal computers, the Apple II was contained in plastic casing to look almost like a typewriter. It was the first computer with a keyboard built in.

Jobs presents the Apple II in 1977

More important, it featured the first-ever color graphics. Here was another feat of technical brilliance, Woz style. Other techies believed you couldn't hook up a color TV because it would require a whole additional memory board to run it, making the computer much too expensive for home use. Woz realized that he could divert some unused memory from the microprocessor itself, the central brain of the computer. But instead of trying to wangle the microprocessor to run the color TV, he flipped the entire concept on its head and made the TV run the microprocessor instead. This crazy trick of engineering snapped the ties that connected personal computers to old-fashioned mainframes. From then on, personal computers weren't just baby mainframes. They were the Wild West, a new technological frontier.

For the Apple II, Woz also designed the personal computer's first floppy-disk drive so that users could easily store information and carry it from one computer to another.

Unlike the Apple I, with its raw, electronic insides on display, the Apple II looked like a sleek appliance. This was no rough, do-it-yourself device that only a computer genius could love. This, as Jobs liked to say, was a computer "for the rest of us."

Given Life by a Killer

The Apple II was a success in computer circles, but those circles were still small in 1978. Apple had great hardware but little software. If you imagine the computer as a human being, the hardware is its body, the microprocessor is its brain, and the operating system is its central nervous system—relaying messages between the brain and the body. Software applications are all of the thoughts and ideas in that brain. Software is what enables a computer to do things—to help you write papers or calculate numbers, create pictures or compose music. Without great software, a computer, no matter how brilliantly designed, just kind of . . . sits there.

The Apple II needed a "killer app" to stay alive. A "killer app" is what hackers call a software application that is so great that it makes the computer that runs it irresistible to hundreds of thousands of new users.

In 1979 the Apple II got what it needed in a software program called VisiCalc—for Visible Calculator. It was a spreadsheet program that allowed you to keep track of many columns of numbers at once.

Imagine, for example, you were budgeting your spending money, month by month, for a year. You would make twelve columns and enter the amount of money for each thing you wanted to buy in the month you wanted to buy it. The VisiCalc program would keep track of the monthly totals and the total for the year. Better yet, if you needed to change one of the numbers, the program automatically changed all the other numbers that were dependent on it, fixing your math without you having to do any calculations or type in numbers all over again.

This may not sound so exciting, considering all the fireworks of computing today, but back then it was a breakthrough. It made the computer incredibly useful to individuals and businesspeople everywhere.

With the help of VisiCalc, the Apple II became the best-selling computer in the world. Apple Computer became one of the fastest-growing companies of all time, and Jobs and Wozniak became multimillionaires. They became famous, too. Steve Jobs appeared, sitting cross-legged and barefoot, in a feature in *Time* magazine. He was only twenty-five years old and already one of the greatest entrepreneurs in business history.

Apple, led by the handsome, irreverent Jobs, stood for a new kind of corporation. They didn't wear coats and ties; they wore jeans, shorts, and sneakers. They didn't work an eight-hour day from nine to five. They worked fourteen-hour days that started at noon and didn't end until well after midnight.

They didn't work that hard because they had to. They worked that hard because they wanted to. Their work was their lives. They were changing the world, building the coolest computers, hacking the best code. And they were having a lot of fun, too.

Their glory was cemented in 1980, when Apple Computer first sold stock to the public—allowing anyone in the world with some extra money to buy a piece of Apple. People went crazy for it. It seemed everybody wanted to own a little bit of the garage-grown techie revolution. And the demand for shares of Apple sent the price of the stock soaring. As the founders, Steve Jobs and Steve Wozniak owned more shares of stock than anybody. They were, all of a sudden, very, very rich young men.

A Taste of Competition

The executives at the giant IBM Corporation couldn't help but notice what the two boys from California had done with the personal computer. IBM took pride in being

The IBM PC as it looked in 1981

the biggest, best computer maker by far, and they certainly didn't want Steve Jobs and Steve Wozniak changing that. IBM had believed, like many others, that big, mainframe computers were the only kind of serious computers and that these small computers were just for techies and hobbyists. But now they saw Apple, and they knew they were wrong. And if personal computers were going to be popular, then IBM was going to be the company to sell them.

In 1981, IBM introduced its PC. Goliath was getting into the boxing ring with David. Steve Jobs wasn't scared, though. He was confident and brash to begin with, and his great success at Apple only made him more so. In honor of the launch of IBM's PC, Jobs took out teasing full-page ads in newspapers across the country that read: "Welcome, IBM. Seriously."

As expected, the IBM personal computer made a very big splash. And more than that, IBM made the personal computer serious business. Forget the long-haired hackers, Homebrew hobbyists, and California hippies. IBM built safe, functional PCs that made businesspeople all over the country feel comfy.

IBM's PC was an instant success, quickly becoming the fastest-selling personal computer. It was especially popular with businesspeople, who trusted the IBM name.

But IBM's executives were in such a hurry to mix it up with Apple that they made a couple of mistakes they would later deeply regret.

The entry of IBM into the personal computer game would change the fate of Apple forever, but not in exactly the way you might think. Yes, IBM set the standard for PCs from that moment forward, but they didn't reap the rewards and success and money. . . . Well, not as much as you might imagine. Who did?

Microsoft. But all that came a little later.

CHAPTER THREE

The Macintosh: A Love Story

A Walk in the PARC

STEVE JOBS BELIEVED THERE WAS ONE WAY TO COMPETE WITH IBM—AND EVERYBODY ELSE FOR THAT MATTER: MAKE A COMPUTER A MILLION TIMES BETTER THAN ANYBODY ELSE'S.

BUT IT WASN'T AS SIMPLE AS TEAMING UP WITH HIS PAL WOZ AGAIN. WOZ HAD BECOME LESS INTERESTED IN THE DAY-TO-DAY RUNNING OF A BUSINESS AND IN 1981 CRASHED HIS SMALL AIRPLANE WHILE PRACTICING LANDINGS AT A LOCAL AIRPORT. WOZ WASN'T BADLY INJURED, BUT HE DID SPEND SEVERAL WEEKS RECOVERING FROM AMNESIA. AND AFTER THAT, HIS heart wasn't in Apple anymore. He went back to Berkeley to finish his college degree and pursue his interest in teaching. This time Jobs had to look elsewhere for technical inspiration.

The seed for the Macintosh was planted in 1979, in a meeting that would forever change the way we relate to our computers. Jobs and a few of his engineers were offered a look inside a place called Xerox PARC—which stands for Palo Alto Research Center. Palo Alto was the home of Stanford University and one of the most dynamic spots in Silicon Valley.

Xerox, the mammoth copier company, had started PARC as a center for advanced, futuristic research. They hired a bunch of great scientists and told them to design "the office of the future." The scientists loved Xerox PARC because they had complete freedom to dream up whatever ideas they felt like without pressure to make or sell anything. As a result, they came up with some incredible things—computer networking, the mouse, the laser printer, and the ability to display pictures and graphics on-screen rather than just numbers and letters.

Unfortunately for the scientists at PARC, though, its parent company, Xerox, never saw or understood the value of what they were doing. Xerox never built any products around

PARC's groundbreaking technology. If they had, Xerox would probably now be the biggest name in technology—the leaders in computers, printers, the Internet . . . you name it. Instead they stuck with copying.

Xerox didn't see the value of the exciting things going on at PARC, but in two brief visits Steve Jobs did. He got to see a demonstration of the Alto computer, with its graphical user interface (GUI—pronounced "gooey") and mouse, and beautiful graphics, and his mind was blown. They were light-years ahead of everybody else.

You see, at that time nobody communicated with their computer through graphics the way we do now. Nobody used a mouse. In the old days, in order to communicate with your computers, you had to type in commands.

For example, if you wanted to check your floppy disk for a file, you would type: DIR[space]a:\myfiles.

The Xerox Alto in 1974, a computer far ahead of its time

Computer users had to read fat instruction manuals and memorize symbols and commands in order to do basic things like print a page or save their work.

So when Jobs saw at PARC a computer screen filled with friendly icons—or pictures—pull-down menus, and overlapping windows all controlled by the click of a mouse, he couldn't believe it. It had the look and feel of a real desktop. We take the GUI for granted now, but for Jobs in 1979 it was mind-boggling.

From that day forward Jobs knew how the future of computing would look. His goal in starting Apple was to build a computer "for the rest of us," for ordinary people who didn't know programming languages. The scientists at Xerox PARC demonstrated the ultimate user-friendly computer experience and provided the spark for Jobs's beloved Macintosh.

Hello, Macintosh

At the time, Jobs had been working on a computer called the Lisa, named for his baby daughter. But once he saw what was happening at PARC, he grew impatient with the Lisa's capabilities and the slowness of the project. Jobs was so frustrated, he started driving everybody crazy. He got himself kicked off the Lisa team.

Nearly everyone who meets Steve Jobs describes him as passionate. They say he is almost supernaturally good at making you believe what he believes. He has striking looks, a challenging expression, and a rare dexterity with words. There is a famous saying among people who know him that Jobs is surrounded by a "reality distortion field." He is so dazzling and so persuasive that he almost seems to bend reality to his point of view. According to people who have worked with him, he is so intense and hardworking, he can be inspiring if you agree with him and exhausting if you don't. And he did not agree with the other members of the Lisa team.

He left Lisa and poured all of his passion and energy into designing the Macintosh, a computer that he promised the world would be "insanely great."

He wanted to make sure the Mac embodied all the thrilling things he had seen at PARC. He couldn't look inside the Alto to see exactly how the PARC engineers had done it, but he knew it

The Lisa

could be done, and that's all that mattered. He had his vision now, and he was unstoppable.

He formed a team of the best and brightest engineers and programmers he could find and worked them to the bone. Jobs is famous for pushing people as far as their creativity and brainpower can possibly carry them and then pushing them harder. Jobs told his Mac development team they were going to "put a dent in the universe." As he later explained to a *New York Times* reporter, "The Macintosh turned out so well because the people working on it were musicians, artists, poets, and historians who also happened to be excellent computer scientists."

Jobs never liked anything that was conventional or ordinary, so he urged his team to be outrageous, revolutionary, even if it meant shocking or upsetting people. He knew that change was almost necessarily unsettling, and change was exactly what he wanted. He made his design team feel like outlaws and even flew a pirate flag over the building where they worked. It pictured a skull and crossbones, but instead of the eye was the multicolored apple. "It's better to be a pirate than to join the navy," Jobs would say.

The Macintosh team became the elite, cool kids on the Apple campus. They had their own building, their own concert grand piano, their own fresh fruit juices in the refrigerator, and their own state-of-the-art video games to play when they needed to let off a little steam.

Jobs actually encouraged the competition between the Macintosh team and the Apple II and Lisa teams. Even though the Apple II was by far their best-selling computer—the product that kept the whole company going—Jobs made the Apple II scientists feel second best. Legend has it that one Apple party turned into a big, ugly food fight between the Macintosh and the Apple II teams. Jobs felt that this competition helped motivate his team, but other executives at Apple thought that it was just plain divisive.

After five intense, grueling years Jobs and his team had

completed their masterpiece. The Macintosh truly was a feat of brilliance. It was the most stylish, complete, user-friendly computer of its time, arriving with its built-in screen, its components pre-assembled, and its software pre-loaded. You just needed to plug it in. And when you did, you were greeted by a little icon in the middle of

Jobs's beloved Macintosh. The original.

your screen—a picture of a smiling Mac.

At the Mac's debut demonstration in 1984 at the Flint Center auditorium of Cupertino College, Jobs wore a rare suit and unveiled his offspring with immense pride. "Hello," the computer said, the word spreading out in curvy script over the screen. The monitor then came alive with icons and simple pull-down menus.

On other computers, when you wanted to delete a file, you typed:

JOHN DONOVAN LIBRARY
MADISON CENTRAL SCHOOL
Madison, New York 1 402

DEL[space]a:\myfiles\myfile.doc

On the Macintosh you dragged a little picture of your file to the little picture of a trash can, and it was done. There was a feeling with the Macintosh that you didn't need to learn how to communicate with it. It had learned how to communicate with you. Most computers felt like machines, and to many the Macintosh felt like a friend.

Now Jobs was ready to introduce his pride and joy to the public, and he did it with what is probably the most famous TV commercial in history. It was one minute long and ran only one time, during the Super Bowl in January 1984. It was based on George Orwell's classic novel *1984*, published in 1949, in which Orwell imagined a bleak future where people had no freedom or privacy. It showed a brightly dressed female athlete sprinting into an auditorium filled with grim, gloomy workers hypnotized by their leader, speaking to them from a screen at the front of the giant room. Chased by storm troopers, the athlete hurls a sledgehammer at the screen, shattering it and obliterating the leader's face. The idea was that the Macintosh could free people from the drab monotony of technology like the

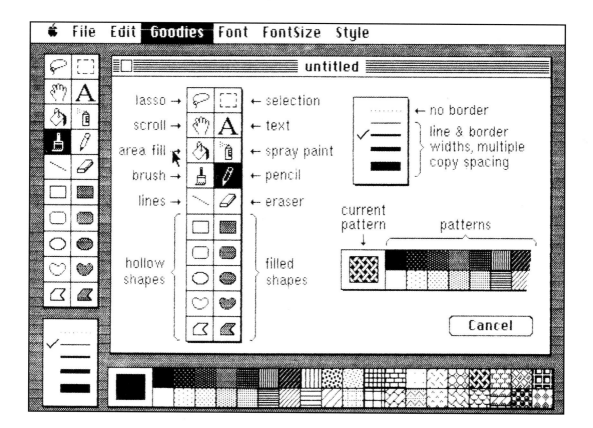

A look at the Mac's GUI

kind IBM offered. IBM represented oppression, and Macintosh represented freedom and creativity.

The commercial made a big impact. Chances are, any person over the age of thirty you ask will remember that ad. Later it was voted Best Ad of All Time by *Adweek* magazine. The IBM management probably wasn't so happy about it, but Steve Jobs had made his dream come true.

A Fateful Decision

In 1983, while he was working away on his Macintosh, Steve Jobs decided that Apple needed an experienced businessperson to help run the company. Jobs was still in his twenties and a visionary, not a seasoned businessman. When he met John Sculley, an important executive at Pepsi, Jobs felt he had found his man. But Sculley wasn't interested in the job at first. He lived on the East Coast and resisted moving his family to California. Jobs used his powers of persuasion on Sculley, reportedly saying to him: "Do you want to spend your life selling sugared water— or do you want to come with me and change the world?" Sculley

Steve Jobs, John Sculley, and Steve Wozniak in 1984

could hardly turn that down. So he joined Apple as its president that same year.

At first the men got along perfectly. Jobs was eager to learn about big business and marketing. Sculley was captivated by Jobs's grasp of technology. But people inside Apple started to complain about Jobs and his Macintosh team. Executives and investors saw the divisions in the company egged on by the hard-driving Jobs and told Sculley they feared Jobs was out of control.

The Problem with Incompatibility

It might have turned out all right if the Macintosh had been the blazing success that Jobs predicted. But it wasn't. At least not at first. The first Macintosh, for all its friendliness and charm, had some big failings. It was slow, and the design made it hard to expand the amount of memory to speed it up. Jobs loved the mouse so much that he made it so the Mac didn't allow users to control the cursor from the keyboard at all. Besides that, it came with a low-quality printer that couldn't print fine enough documents for most businesses. Businesses spent by far the most money on buying new computers, and they felt that the Macintosh was friendly and cute, but it wasn't businesslike. The worst problem, though, was that there just weren't many software applications for the new computer.

Over time, Apple engineers would find a way to fix and improve nearly all the problems with the Macintosh. And they would soon find salvation in a single application. But the general problem of software never went away. That's because most software development is done by third-party companies independent of Apple or IBM. Microsoft has become the most famous, but there are thousands of others creating games and programs to make a computer not just entertaining, not just useful, but also essential to our lives.

There was one crucial reason why software developers weren't making software for the Mac, and that was IBM.

TECH TALK

Interpreted Languages vs. Compiled Languages

Once a program is written, it needs to be compiled. Compiling a program means translating it from a programmer's language into a machine language—a code based on ones and zeros, switching the flow of electricity through the transistors on or off. Computers can only understand machine languages, and people have a very hard time reading and writing in them. Luckily, the compiler translates between man and machine. Using a compiler, a programmer can write complex tasks for a computer without knowing any machine language directly.

Some languages are compiled right after a program is written. These are called compiled languages. If this is done, the program can be used any time and never has to be translated again. The disadvantage is that once the program is compiled on a particular computer, it starts using the machine language of that computer. If you compile on a Macintosh, your program then runs only on a Macintosh. Some examples of compiled languages are C and C++

Interpreted languages are compiled only when a program runs. The advantage of this built-in compiling is that the program language can be used anywhere. It can run on Macintosh, Windows, Linux, or virtually any operating system. The disadvantage is that interpreted programs are slower. They need to compile and run, rather than just run. Some examples of interpreted languages are Java and Perl.

When IBM had taken the computer world by storm with its PC in 1981, they had introduced what's called an open architecture. That means they assembled their PC out of parts that anybody could get. Furthermore, IBM was in such a hurry that they didn't have enough time to build an operating system (OS) from the ground up. An operating system connects the hardware of the computer to its software, and it is both critically important and hugely complicated. In order to save time, they needed to buy one, so they called up a young man named Bill Gates at a little software company called Microsoft. Microsoft didn't even have an operating system, but they sure didn't want to turn away a big client like IBM. So they ran across town to Seattle Computer Products and bought one called Q-DOS or Quick and Dirty Operating System—even though it was basically a knockoff of a more established OS called CP/M. Microsoft only paid about $50,000 for a system that would earn them billions.

That's when IBM made what's been called the $100 billion mistake. They agreed to license Microsoft's software—meaning IBM would pay Microsoft every time they bundled Microsoft's products with one of their new computers. But they never asked to license it exclusively. That meant Microsoft not only made a lot of money selling their software on every single computer IBM sold, but they also could sell that very same software to anybody else who would pay for it.

Because of IBM's open architecture and the fact that they used Microsoft software, any company could make a computer exactly like the best-selling IBM PC. And plenty of companies did. They made what are called IBM clones, meaning their computers did exactly what the IBM computers did, ran all the same software programs the IBMs ran, but often cost a lot less. Young companies like Compaq and Gateway stole the show, and IBM was such an enormous, slow-moving company that they could hardly compete. Suddenly Compaq was selling more computers than Apple or even IBM!

Bill Gates in 1983

There was one thing that all of these computers had in common: Microsoft software. In this new age of the PC, software was rapidly becoming more important than hardware, and Microsoft was king.

What did all this mean for Apple? It meant that Apple was slowly being left out in the cold. The IBM PCs and all the millions of clones all ran the exact same software, and the Apple didn't. It ran on its own system, which was different and incompatible. Microsoft became the standard platform, and that meant all the software developers wrote for that standard. Fewer and fewer of them wanted to develop software for Apple. It became a vicious circle: The fewer programs there were, the fewer customers bought Apple, and the fewer customers there were for Apple, the less the programmers felt like writing software for them.

Apple, with its constantly improving Macintosh, had one really big advantage that kept it in business. Its interface was simply better than that of the Microsoft clones. The Mac OS was way ahead of what Microsoft had (though in time that would change). The Mac was more efficient and much easier to use. Even most clone buyers agreed that the Mac was better and that its GUI was light-years ahead of the plodding, text-based DOS interface. But those clone buyers needed compatibility, and they needed all that software being written for them.

In 1985, what the Mac desperately needed was its own

killer app. Thanks to Jobs and an investment he had made in a little company called Adobe, that killer app was on its way. But it would come too late to save Steve Jobs.

A Heartbreaking Moment

In the spring of 1985 the Mac was faltering, and Apple was losing ground to the IBM clones. John Sculley and Apple's board of directors—the small group of business experts responsible for guiding the company—were getting nervous. The person who made them most nervous was Steve Jobs. Jobs was so proud of his Macintosh, that he couldn't concede that it was not selling nearly as well as he had predicted. He simply would not accept the sales numbers. But this was one piece of reality Jobs couldn't bend. Apple was losing money for the first time.

In April of that year Sculley had a secret meeting with the board of directors and told them he wanted to take away all of Jobs's responsibilities at Apple. Furthermore, Sculley told them, if they didn't agree, he was going to quit.

Jobs heard about what was happening and called each of

the board members to ask for their support. On May 24, Sculley called an emergency meeting of the board. He told the board that Jobs had to go. Then Jobs told the group that Sculley was bad for Apple, that it was Sculley who should go. The decision was left up to the board—would they choose Sculley or Jobs? Every member picked Jobs.

The board saw Sculley as safe, businesslike, grown up, predictable. They believed Jobs was too temperamental and erratic to run a big, important company.

Jobs was bitterly hurt. Apple Computer was his life. That year he told a reporter, "You've probably had somebody punch you in the stomach and it knocks the wind out of you and you cannot breathe. The harder you try to breathe, the more you cannot breathe. And you know that the only thing you can do is just relax so you can start breathing again."

Technically, Jobs hadn't been fired, but he'd been stripped of his power and given no projects to work on. He needed a purpose to thrive, and he had none. Finally, in September, he packed up his things and sold every share of his Apple stock but one. In leaving Apple at the age of thirty, he was leaving his true love, his career, and his home.

CHAPTER FOUR

What Happened NeXT

Pixar

JOBS THREW HIMSELF INTO TWO BIG BUSINESS VENTURES AFTER APPLE. ONE WAS A GIGANTIC SUCCESS. THE OTHER WASN'T . . . BUT IT LED HIM TO SOMETHING REMARKABLE.

THE FIRST WAS A LITTLE COMPANY CALLED PIXAR. GEORGE LUCAS, LEGENDARY PRODUCER OF THE *STAR WARS* MOVIES, OWNED IT AS PART OF INDUSTRIAL LIGHT AND MAGIC, HIS SPECIAL-EFFECTS COMPANY. BY 1986, LUCAS WANTED TO SPIN OFF THE COMPANY, AND JOBS WAS EAGER TO BUY IT. JOBS WAS FLUSH WITH MONEY FROM HIS SALE OF APPLE STOCK, SO HE had no trouble paying the $10 million that George Lucas had asked. Over the next few years Jobs spent another $50 million of his own money developing the most advanced, cutting-edge computer animation.

Animation had traditionally been done by pencil on paper, though since the 1970s more and more of the busy, technical work was being done on computers. Most artists and animators feared that computers would kill the creativity and the quirky specialness of a real artist's hand. Jobs and his computer graphics experts disagreed. They believed the computer could unleash a whole new level of imagination, empowering artists to do more than they ever could before. They believed that all the animation could be designed and drawn on the computer, and they proved it in 1988 with a short film called *Tin Toy*. It was the first computer-animated film to win an Academy Award.

Pixar's giant masterpiece took many years to complete. As usual, Jobs and his team, including brilliant animator and director John Lasseter, wanted every second of the full-length movie to be perfect. It was called *Toy Story*, and it premiered in 1995 to fantastic reviews from critics everywhere. It wasn't only that the technology was mind-boggling to animators and computer scientists, although it certainly was. More important, the characters—Woody and Buzz Lightyear—were lovably human, and the story was old-fashioned and irresistible.

Once again Jobs displayed his brilliance for imagining in technology not so much what appealed to people's minds, but to their hearts. For him, as always, technology was a means to an end, never the end itself. He saw the computer as an inspiration to do things more easily, certainly, but more important, to do things better. To free the imagination, never to replace it.

Toy Story was an instant hit. It went on to be the third most successful animated movie of all time, right behind *The Lion King* and *Aladdin*. Toys, books, and music based on the movie were selling like crazy. Suddenly everybody in the movie business knew about Pixar. Steve Jobs had done it again. When he offered the public the opportunity to buy shares in the company, they jumped at the chance. Suddenly his $60 million investment was worth more than $1 billion.

Three years later Pixar came out with *A Bug's Life*, which became another giant hit, and one year after that, the sequel to *Toy Story*, called *Toy Story 2*. Pixar had made only three

JOHN DONOVAN LIBRARY
MADISON CENTRAL SCHOOL
Madison, New York 13402

full-length movies, and every one of them was a runaway success with critics and audiences all over the world. All three are among the top-ten most successful animated films of all time.

Pixar's next project is a movie called *Monsters, Inc.*, and if the past is any lesson, it, too, will make animation history.

NeXT

Steve Jobs's other big business venture after Apple was called NeXT Computer. He started the company in 1986, the same year he bought Pixar, with a few of his favorite engineers from Apple. Once again he needed technical inspiration to drive his ambition, and once again it came from the brilliant research done at Xerox PARC.

In an interview with a writer named Bob Cringely for a television documentary called *Triumph of the Nerds*, Jobs said that when he made the famous visit to Xerox PARC in 1979, he saw three astonishing things. But he was so blinded by the first thing that he virtually missed the other two. Until later, that is.

The first thing was the GUI—the graphical user interface, which inspired the Macintosh and a copycat system called Windows. (More on that a little later.) It's clear how deeply that one affected Jobs's life and career.

The second thing was the ethernet, a system connecting all the computers in the Xerox PARC office, developed by an engineer named Bob Metcalfe. The ethernet was an early precursor to the modern-day Internet, which exploded onto the scene in 1994, when a young hacker named Marc Andreessen popularized the browser. Just imagine if Steve Jobs had been paying attention to that in 1979.

But he wasn't.

The third thing he saw was more subtle, but for him at least as profound. It was called object-oriented programming. Traditional software systems, like Microsoft Windows, for example, form one interconnected whole, in which all the functions are tied in with all the other functions. The idea behind object-oriented programming is to create a system of software "objects" that can be plugged in or removed without affecting the rest of the system. It's almost like the difference between a rug and a quilt. A rug is usually woven together as

TECH TALK

Procedural Languages

There are many styles of programming languages used today. A programmer uses these languages to explain to a computer exactly what tasks to perform. When you get down to it, programs are just lists of tasks for the computer to carry out, but there are a lot of different ways to explain those tasks. The oldest and probably still the most common kind of programming language is called procedural.

In a procedural language, a programmer tells the computer what to do, step by step. For example, if you wanted the computer to write the word "HELLO" on the screen, you would give it one instruction at a time until the job was done.

1) write the letter H
2) write the letter E
3) write the letter L
4) write the letter L
5) write the letter O

Some languages that use a procedural style are called Perl, C, and Cobol.

TECH TALK

Object-Oriented Languages

Another style of programming language is called object-oriented. Instead of writing a program, programmers make objects. An object is a representation of a thing or place or concept.

For example, you could make an object to represent a letter. Then you could make a word object that would hold a bunch of letter objects. Then you could make a printer object that printed this word.

```
    Word
    _____
    | (letter) H   |
    | (letter) E   |        _____
    | (letter) L   | ----------------------> | Printer |
    | (letter) L   |        _____
    | (letter) O   |
    _____
```

There are several advantages of doing things this way. First, once you've made an object, you can use it many times in many different places. For example, after creating this program you can use the letter object, the word object, and the printer object again in many different places. Some languages that use an object-oriented style are Java, C++, and Smalltalk.

one big piece, with every thread connecting to every other thread. A quilt, on the other hand, is typically made up of little squares of fabric sewn together. If you want to change or add to the pattern of a rug, you would have to unravel it all and start from scratch. If you want to change a quilt, you could just remove some of the squares and add new ones.

Jobs recognized that object-oriented programming could make it easier to upgrade a software program—to add exciting new "pieces" or functions without having to build the whole system from the ground up. He felt that this would also allow all kinds of third-party, independent software developers to build and add on their own little expert pieces of software without having to tie them into the larger operating system. This way a giant software company like Microsoft wouldn't have such a huge advantage—because as it is now, Microsoft owns the Windows operating system, and so they have control over the functions and applications that fit into it.

Jobs may have missed object-oriented programming in favor of the "gooey" when he visited PARC in 1979, but somehow the notion stuck with him. In 1986 it became the spark for his new dream computer, NeXT.

The NeXT computer

Jobs and his engineers worked for three years before they unveiled their masterpiece at a big, splashy event in San Francisco in 1989. It was a sleek black cube, 12 inches (30 centimeters) on a side, containing NeXTstep, the most cutting-edge operating system available and a more elegant, user-friendly interface than even the Mac.

Pretty much all the computer experts agreed that the NeXT was a triumph of technology. It came to be loved by software developers and programmers. In fact, a British scientist named Tim Berners-Lee invented the World Wide Web on a NeXT computer.

But NeXT wasn't a raging commercial success. Not even close.

Sometimes the best technology doesn't win. And that can be a tough pill to swallow, especially if you're Steve Jobs.

Why didn't NeXT succeed? For the same reason that his Macintosh ran into trouble. Microsoft established the standard operating system that more than 85 percent of personal computers ran on—first with DOS and then Windows—and NeXT wasn't part of it. It, like the Macintosh, seemed an orphan.

Microsoft was like the McDonald's of software. Consumers were familiar with it, comfortable with it; it was available cheaply everywhere, no matter where they were. And who can resist those french fries? Who cares if they aren't exactly gourmet food? A giant like McDonald's can make it hard for the little restaurant next door to compete, no matter how delicious their stuff tastes. That's just the way it was with Microsoft and a brand-new system like NeXT.

If you wanted that cutting-edge NeXTstep operating system, you had to buy the NeXT computer, and that cost about $10,000. Besides, if you were already a computer owner, you most likely had to throw away your whole Microsoft-compatible system and all your software applications that went with it. Like the Mac, NeXT's incompatibility made software developers hesitant to write applications for it, even though they admired the system.

By 1993, Jobs realized that the NeXTstep operating system was never going to attract millions of users if it was only available with NeXT hardware. So he made the decision to stop making the hardware—the actual computer—and NeXT would just concentrate on the software. But by this time NeXT had lost a lot of its momentum and confidence. And there was still the problem of McDonald's next door.

NeXTstep was a first-rate operating system, orphaned by the PC clones and its own hardware. Meanwhile, a short distance away was a computer company with huge hardware capabilities desperately in need of a good operating system.

Which computer company? Apple, of course.

Apple Minus Steve Jobs

It was painful for Jobs to leave Apple in 1985, and it was painful for many people inside Apple to see him go. On the day John Sculley announced the news to three thousand employees, several members of the Macintosh team cried right then and there. Jobs might have been prone to temper and troublemaking, but he was also the motivator, the visionary, and the one who simply cared more than anybody else.

Which isn't to say that Apple went down the tubes right away. In fact, five years after Steve Jobs left the company in 1985, Apple was doing better than it ever had before. But its success was due mostly to the plans Jobs had laid before he left, particularly the deal with the tiny company called Adobe.

Thanks to Adobe, the Mac, like the Apple II before it, was the lucky recipient of a genuine "killer app." That killer app was called PostScript, and like so many other things, it had its roots in Xerox PARC. It was the result of technology developed by a computer scientist named John Warnock.

PostScript was software that enabled a computer to communicate with its printer in a new way. Using principles of photocopying technology, it enabled the computer to store and reproduce, with the help of a laser printer, what was designed on the computer exactly as it appeared on screen.

Before PostScript, the very best computer printers worked more or less like typewriters. They were limited to what typewriters could do—letters and numbers in one font, or style, and maybe one or two sizes. And the truth was, most computer printouts looked much worse than documents written on a typewriter.

PostScript changed all that. It made it possible to print pictures and graphics as well as all kinds of numbers and letters and symbols in thousands of different fonts and sizes. PostScript ushered in a new standard known as WYSIWYG, literally pronounced "whizzywig," for "what you see is what you get." That means your printout looks exactly like your document on screen.

Steve Jobs loved this technology the first time he saw it in 1983 and convinced the Apple board to invest $2.5 million to buy 15 percent of the baby company, Adobe. Apple's board moaned and groaned at the time, but it turned out to have been a very smart investment.

Together Adobe and Apple created the phenomenon known as desktop publishing. It not only revolutionized traditional businesses, but it also turned every person with a laser printer and a Mac into a designer and publisher. The Mac, with its graphical interface, made a marriage of pictures and words, and PostScript allowed users to celebrate the wedding in three dimensions—books, magazines, pamphlets, papers, comics, packages . . . anything with words and pictures on paper.

Happily married to its killer app, the Macintosh sold widely. It became the only computer for anybody with an interest in graphics. Macintosh owners were passionate about their computers. They spawned a whole movement fueled by clubs and magazines and newsletters.

The soaring Mac was just the thing Steve Jobs had dreamed of. But he wasn't there to enjoy it.

Mac vs. Windows

In those five years after Steve Jobs left Apple, the Mac had no competition. There were still those IBM clones running on creaky old Microsoft DOS, of course, but the Mac was the only computer sporting the "gooey." While Mac users were happily pointing and clicking, clone users were still typing in commands. The IBM clones were the standard, but many people believed that the Mac, with its PostScript software, was so superior that it would be just a matter of time before it took over the PC world.

Apple Computer corporate headquarters in Cupertino, California

Many computer and business experts believe that the Mac really would have taken over if Apple had licensed their operating system the way Microsoft had done. What if Mac let other computer companies buy the right to use their software so they, too, could get the look and feel of the Mac? What if consumers could have the benefits of the Mac on any computer they chose—Gateway, Compaq, Dell, IBM—no matter how cheap or simple? If everybody was using the Mac platform, then all the third-party software developers would make their games and applications for them instead of the clones. Even Bill Gates, back in 1985, recommended to Apple that they license their superior software and attempt to beat out the IBM clones to become the standard.

But time after time the executives running Apple, John Sculley and Jean-Louis Gassee, decided against licensing. They felt that their Mac was too special, too important to share, even though it probably would have made them a bundle.

It became clear to everyone, including Bill Gates, that the Mac represented the future of personal computing. And if Apple wasn't going to make it happen, then he would.

Slowly but surely, Bill Gates and his programmers at

Microsoft worked on their new operating system called Windows. The first few versions were poor, but it kept getting better. The better it got, the more it looked like the Mac. The first decent version was called Windows 3.0 and was launched in 1990 with lots of fanfare from Microsoft. It had many features the Mac had—pull-down windows, a mouse. But it sat on top of the old DOS operating system, which made it clunky. Version 3.1 came out in 1992 and was better still.

Apple had almost a ten-year technology lead on Microsoft, but the programmers at Microsoft toiled hard to make up the distance. The Mac virtually stood still, becoming more and more removed from the rest of the PC world as Windows overtook it. Apple saw what was happening, but they seemed powerless to stop it. They sued Microsoft for $5.5 billion, claiming that Microsoft had stolen their intellectual property. The lawsuit went on for years, but the court finally decided in Microsoft's favor. For one thing, the Microsoft lawyers claimed that it was all right for them to borrow from the Mac because the Mac team had borrowed from the engineers at Xerox PARC.

As Windows got closer and closer to the Mac, the Mac

became less and less special. Sales at Apple turned downward, while the rest of the computer industry grew at record pace. Apple officially entered hard times.

In 1995, Microsoft launched Windows 95. This was their masterpiece. At last they had gotten rid of DOS and created a true graphical interface on a par with Apple. They advertised it and marketed it more heavily than any computer product in history, claiming its graphical interface was revolutionary. The Mac faithful were not amused. But Windows 95 sold faster and better than anything before it.

It was another nail in the coffin for Apple.

A Decaying Apple

By the end of 1996 the once great Apple Computer was on the verge of collapse. They were losing money fast, and the value of their stock was plummeting. When things started going wrong in the early 1990s, the board fired the chief executive officer (CEO), John Sculley, the very man who had gotten rid of Steve Jobs. They had brought in a new one, Michael

Spindler, but he lasted only a bit over two years. In 1996, as the company descended into a terrible state, they had brought in a man named Gil Amelio to lead Apple.

The biggest problem facing Apple was that their technology had stood still for years in the face of the ever-

Gil Amelio, Apple CEO dethroned by Jobs's return

advancing Microsoft. Windows was getting better and better every year, and Macintosh was still running on an operating system left over from 1985—back in the days when Jobs was still forging the way. Apple knew they were probably heading for extinction if they couldn't come up with a new, improved operating system. Over the years they had tried to build a new system. They had one big project code-named Taligent, another named Pink, and a last one called Copland. Nobody at Apple could decide just how far-reaching the new system needed to be. They couldn't figure out how to make it both dazzlingly new and yet backward-looking enough to stay compatible with its old products—so owners of older Macs could upgrade, too. Each attempt got bogged down in disagreements and indecision.

Most experts agreed that Apple was doomed. The company would keep losing money until it went out of business. Sure, there were still hordes of Mac faithful, but even they agreed that Apple was a dying cause. The beloved patient was terminal. It was just a matter of time.

By 1996 the time bomb was ticking loudly, and money was flying out the door. Apple lost more than a billion dollars in a single year. Apple needed a new operating system in a last gasp at survival, but they no longer had time to build one. That meant they needed to borrow or buy one. It was pretty humiliating for Apple Computer to be looking outside for an operating system. One reporter compared it to General Motors needing to look outside for car engines. The Mac operating system was Apple's pride and joy, its claim to fame.

Ellen Hancock, Apple's chief technology officer, was

forced to consider a lot of unhappy options. She even briefly considered licensing a version of Windows from Microsoft! But one day she got a call from two executives at NeXT, suggesting that she consider their operating system. She was interested. In December 1996 she set up a meeting with Apple CEO Gil Amelio and . . . you guessed it, Steve Jobs.

Jobs walked onto the Apple campus for the first time in eleven years. He himself gave the demonstration of the NeXTstep operating system to the executives at Apple. The Apple team was impressed. Jobs hadn't lost a step. If anything, he had become more of a master at creating excitement around a new technology. Jobs suggested that instead of buying or licensing the NeXT system, Apple should go ahead and buy the whole company. Finally, after some thought, Apple agreed. They bought NeXT Software, Inc., for more than $400 million.

Suddenly, amazingly, Steve Jobs was once again an employee of Apple.

CHAPTER FIVE

Coming Home to Apple

Welcome Home, Steve

On January 7, 1997, at the Macworld convention in San Francisco, the biggest Mac event of the year, Gil Amelio introduced Steve Jobs to an audience of Mac fans four thousand strong. They went crazy. It was the return of a hero. And he was as well-spoken and mesmerizing as ever. They gave him a long, thundering standing ovation. Here, back at Apple, was the true father of the Macintosh. At the end of the presentation Gil Amelio offered another surprise. He invited

Steve Wozniak up onstage, too. Woz wasn't rejoining Apple, but seeing the two Steves together again was a thrilling sight. The crowd went even crazier.

Emotions ran high, and the show was a huge success, but afterward reporters expressed their doubts that anything could save Apple. Steve Jobs had only come on board as a consultant, they said, and what could he really do to help?

A lot, as it turned out.

Saving Apple

People who know Steve Jobs well believed he wouldn't last long as a consultant under Gil Amelio, and they were right.

As Apple continued its downward slide during the first half of 1997, people inside and outside the company got impatient with Amelio's leadership. He wasn't fixing things. In July of that year the board of directors fired him and decided to search for a new CEO. Jobs apparently was offered the job but turned it down, saying to reporter Jim Carlton, "I've already got the best job in the world, which is to be part of the team at

Pixar. The problem is I have a life. I just can't be the CEO of Apple. I just don't have that to give."

Jobs promised to help find the perfect CEO for Apple, and in the meantime he would help guide them until they found the right person. But it seems that Steve Jobs has trouble doing anything partway.

He started making big changes instantly. In a shocking performance as the keynote speaker at the Boston Macworld show in August, he told the crowd that he was getting rid of most of the members of the board and getting new, better ones. But there was a much bigger piece of news. Jobs announced that Apple had made a deal with Microsoft. Microsoft would invest $150 million, much needed in Apple, and Apple would support Microsoft's Internet browser. The loyal Mac users couldn't believe it when a huge screen dropped down to cover the stage and Bill Gates's face appeared from a satellite hookup. Many members of the audience booed, believing still that Microsoft was the evil competition, but Jobs said this: "We have to let go of the notion that for Apple to win, Microsoft has to lose. For Apple to win, Apple has to do a really good job." And the truth was, Apple really did need the help.

Jobs had never been afraid to upset an applecart, and he certainly wasn't now. He decided the changes couldn't wait until they had time to hire a CEO, so he would just have to make them now. He fired people, he discontinued products, he cut costs, and he rebuilt the company from the top down and the bottom up. A lot of people were shaken by the changes and criticized his manner. They felt he was harsh and overly controlling, even a bully sometimes.

Jobs, soon after his return to Apple, in front of a "Think Different" ad

But his changes started making a difference. Within a few months he unveiled an inspiring new advertising campaign with the slogan "Think Different," featuring beautiful black-and-white photographs of controversial, rebellious, troublemaking icons and geniuses of our culture. Legends such as John Lennon, Pablo Picasso, and Albert Einstein. This campaign was a smashing success and placed Apple right back in the spotlight.

At the keynote address at Macworld in January 1998, Jobs gave a speech and a series of demos showing the state of Apple. At the end he began to leave the stage, then stopped. "Oh, one more thing," he said to the audience in an offhand way. "Think profit."

The crowd went wild. After years of steep losses Apple Computer had actually managed to turn a profit of $47 million. Nobody could believe it. Particularly not the financial experts who had claimed that Apple couldn't even hope to break even.

Hello Again

Jobs's next legendary performance came later that year. It was staged at the Flint Center auditorium at Cupertino College, the same place the Macintosh was introduced. As on that night fourteen years earlier, Jobs again wore a rare suit. This time he unveiled his Macintosh reborn, now called the iMac, for Internet Mac. It was a beautiful sight and unlike any computer in the world, blue and translucent white with a rounded, organic, conelike shape and a keyboard that lit up when you touched it. It was by far the coolest, most stylish computer ever built. This time the computer's screen read, "Hello again."

"It looks like it's from another planet, but a good planet," Jobs said to the audience.

The iMac became a runaway success, as did the iBook, the portable version that Apple introduced a year later. In fact, the iBook soon became the

Jobs introduces the iMac in 1998.

best-selling computer of its kind. The sales of the new machines helped push Apple to bigger and bigger profits. The price of Apple stock climbed from $13 to $150.

But guess what? Jobs still wasn't the CEO. He had taken to

calling himself interim CEO—or iCEO—in spite of everybody begging him to take the job for real. He didn't even get paid a salary for all his work. Of course nobody on the board had any interest in looking for a CEO anymore. They had the perfect CEO right there, only he refused to call himself by the title.

It took until the year 2000 for Jobs to finally agree to be the official CEO of Apple, while remaining the CEO of Pixar. At last Jobs has embraced his old love again, and Apple Computer loves him right back.

It's hard to imagine a more satisfying vindication or a bigger triumph for Steve Jobs than his return to Apple. After the company stood still for eleven years, he got it moving again. He showed once and for all that he really is the heart and soul of Apple.

What If?

What would have happened if Steve Jobs had never left Apple in 1985? Would Apple be bigger than Microsoft? Would the Macintosh have won the war of the operating system, as so many people believe it richly deserved to do?

Or did Jobs become a better, smarter businessman in his time away? Did the pain of that experience make him more thoughtful, more circumspect, and better able to achieve what he has today?

It's impossible to know, but it's fun to imagine.

The real question is, would he have even wanted Apple to become the worldwide standard, like Microsoft? Would he have wanted Apple to become the navy rather than stay the rebellious pirate?

Maybe Jobs really did create Apple in his own image. A revolutionary, an underdog, an outsider. Maybe that's exactly how Steve Jobs likes it.

A Family Man

Now Steve Jobs lives in a comfortable redbrick house in Palo Alto, California, in the same valley where he grew up. There aren't many fruit orchards left.

He has another enormous priority in his life besides his

two companies: his family. He lives with his wife, Laurene, their three children, and his older daughter, Lisa, from an earlier relationship. He balances his hectic lives at Apple and Pixar with time at home with his family.

He has forged another set of family ties, too. As an adult he located his biological mother, Joanne Simpson, and discovered he had a biological sister he never knew. Her name is Mona Simpson, and she is a well-known novelist, author of critically praised books such as *Anywhere but Here*. Since they've found each other, they've been close as siblings and friends.

These days Jobs's colleagues and friends describe him as a much mellower, more trusting man than he was two decades before. "He listens a lot more," said Pamela Kerwin, a colleague at Pixar, "and he's more relaxed, more mature."

Jobs told a *New York Times* writer that his goal with respect to his children was "just to try to be as good a father to them as my father was to me. I think about that every day of my life."

Steve Jobs has an incredible legacy to pass on to his children and quite a few great adventures. More than anything, perhaps, he has a legacy of courage. In every professional effort he has displayed the courage to try and try and try some more, no matter what blocks his way. He possesses the remarkable confidence to care deeply and fully, without any sense of timidity or shame.

"And it's the people who are crazy enough to think they can change the world who actually do," said a famous Apple television commercial.

There is a message dear to Steve Jobs's own rebellious heart.

Steve Jobs, 2000

Circles

Not long ago Jobs requested a permit from the city of Palo Alto to buy the land next to his house. He didn't want to build a bigger house or a new house. He wanted to bulldoze the structure that was there and plant a fruit orchard, growing apricots, cherries . . . maybe even apples.

sources and bibliography

Carlton, Jim. *Apple: The Inside Story of Intrigue, Egomania, and Business Blunders.* New York: HarperCollins, 1997.

Cringely, Robert X. *Accidental Empires.* New York: HarperBusiness, 1996.

Freiberger, Paul, and Michael, Swaine. *Fire in the Valley: The Making of the Personal Computer.* New York: McGraw-Hill, 2000.

Kaplan, David A. *The Silicon Boys and Their Valley of Dreams.* New York: HarperCollins, 1999.

Levy, Steven. "Insanely Great: An ode to an artifact, the computer that changed everything." *Wired* magazine, February 1994.

Lohr, Steve. "Creating Jobs." *New York Times*, January 12, 1997.

Malone, Michael S. *Infinite Loop: How the World's Most Insanely Great Computer Company Went Insane.* New York: Doubleday, 1999.

Piller, Charles. "The 50 People Who Most Influenced Business This Century; Woz, Jobs Planted Seeds of a Revolution." *Los Angeles Times*, October 25, 1999.

Young, Jeffrey. *Forbes Greatest Technology Stories: Inspiring Tales of Business.* New York: John Wiley & Sons, Inc. 1998.

index

Photography credits

AP/World Wide Photos, 21, 35, 39, 61, 65, 71, 73; Computer Museum History Centre, 14, 17, 26, 33, 31, 55; Wilson, Doug/Black Star Publishing/PictureQuest, 43.

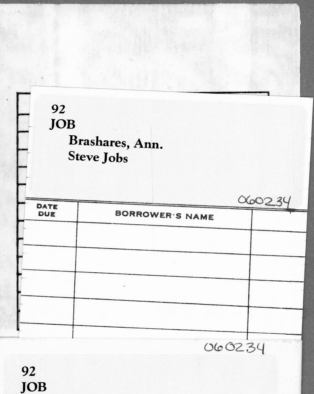

92
JOB
    Brashares, Ann.
    Steve Jobs

060234

DATE DUE	BORROWER'S NAME	

060234

92
JOB
    Brashares, Ann.
    Steve Jobs

JOHN DONOVAN LIBRARY
MADISON CENTRAL SCHOOL
Madison, New York 13402